The Missions: California's Heritage

MISSION SAN FERNANDO REY de ESPAÑA

by

Mary Null Boulé

Merryant Publishers, Inc.
Vashon, WA 98070
206-463-3879

Book Seventeen in a series of twenty-one

With special thanks to Msgr. Francis J. Weber, Archivist of the Los Angeles Catholic Diocese for his encouragement and expertise in developing this series.

This series is dedicated to my sister, Nancy Null Kenyon, whose editing skills and support were so freely given.

Library of Congress Catalog Card Number: 89-90967

ISBN: 1-877599-16-6

Father Junípero Serra

INTRODUCTION

Building of a mission church involved everyone in the mission community. Priests were engineers and architects; Native Americans did the construction. Mission Indian in front is pouring adobe mix into a brick form. Bricks were then dried in the sun.

FATHER SERRA AND THE MISSIONS: AN INTRODUCTION

The year was 1769. On the east coast of what would soon become the United States, the thirteen original colonies were making ready to break away from England. On the west coast of our continent, however, there could be found only untamed land inhabited by Native Americans, or Indians. Although European explorers had sailed up and down the coast in their ships, no one but American Indians had explored the length of this land on foot . . . until now.

To this wild, beautiful country came a group of adventurous men from New Spain, as Mexico was then called. They were following the orders of their king, King Charles III of Spain.

One of the men was a Spanish missionary named Fray Junípero Serra. He had been given a tremendous job; especially since he was fifty-six years old, an old man in those days. King Charles III had ordered mission settlements to be built along the coast of Alta (Upper) California and it was Fr. Serra's task to carry out the king's wishes.

Father Serra had been born in the tiny village of Petra

5

on the island of Mallorca, Spain. He had done such an excellent job of teaching and working with the Indians in Mexican missions, the governor of New Spain had suggested to the king that Fr. Serra do the same with the Indians of Alta California. Hard-working Fray Serra was helped by Don Gaspár de Portolá, newly chosen governor of Alta California, and two other Franciscan priests who had grown up with Fr. Serra in Mallorca, Father Fermin Lasuén and Father Francisco Palóu.

There were several reasons why men had been told to build settlements along the coast of this unexplored country. First, missions would help keep the land as Spanish territory. Spain wanted to be sure the rest of the world knew it owned this rich land. Second, missions were to be built near harbors so towns would grow there. Ships from other countries could then stop to trade with the Spaniards, but these travelers could not try to claim the land for themselves. Third, missions were a good way to turn Indians into Christian, hard-working people.

It would be nice if we could write here that everything went well; that twenty-one missions immediately sprang up along the coast. Unfortunately, all did not go well. It would take fifty-four years to build all the California missions. During those fifty-four years many people died from Indian attacks, sickness, and starvation. Earthquakes and fires constantly ruined mission buildings, which then had to be built all over again. Fr. Serra calmly overcame each problem as it happened, as did those priests who followed him.

When a weary Fray Serra finally died in 1784, he had founded nine missions from San Diego to Monterey and had arranged the building of many more. Fr. Lasuén continued Fr. Serra's work, adding eight more missions to the California mission chain. The remaining four missions were founded in later years.

Originally, plans had been to place missions a hard day's walk from each other. Many of them were really quite far apart. Travelers truly struggled to go from one mission to another along the 650 miles of walking road known as El Camino Real, The Royal Highway. Today keen eyes will sometimes see tall, curved poles with bells hanging from them sitting by the side of streets and highways. These bell poles are marking a part of the old El Camino Real.

At first Spanish soldiers were put in charge of the towns which grew up near each mission. The priests were told to handle only the mission and its properties. It did not take long to realize the soldiers were not kind and gentle leaders. Many were uneducated and did not have the understanding they should have had in dealing with people. So the padres came to be in charge of not only the mission, but of the townspeople and even of the soldiers.

The first missions at San Diego and Monterey were built near the ocean where ships could bring them needed supplies. After early missions began to grow their own food and care for themselves, later mission compounds were built farther away from the coast. What one mission did well, such as leatherworking, candlemaking, or raising cattle, was shared with other missions. As a result, missions became somewhat specialized in certain products.

Although mission buildings looked different from mission to mission, most were built from one basic plan. Usually a compound was constructed as a large, four-sided building with an inner patio in the center. The outside of the quadrangle had only one or two doors, which were locked at night to protect the mission. A church usually sat at one corner of the quadrangle and was always the tallest and largest part of the mission compound.

Facing the inner patio were rooms for the two priests living there, workshops, a kitchen, storage rooms for grain and food, and the mission office. Rooms along the back of the quadrangle often served as home to the unmarried Indian women who worked in the kitchen. The rest of the Indians lived just outside the walls of the mission in their own village.

Beyond the mission wall and next to the church was a cemetery. Today you can still see many of the original headstones of those who died while living and working at the mission. Also outside the walls were larger workshops, a reservoir holding water used at the mission, and orchards containing fruit trees. Huge fields surrounded each mission where crops grew and livestock such as sheep, cattle, and horses grazed.

It took a great deal of time for some Indian tribes to understand the new way of life a mission offered, even though the

Native Americans always had food and shelter when they became mission Indians. Each morning all Indians were awakened at sunrise by a church bell calling them to church. Breakfast followed church . . . and then work. The women spun thread and made clothes, as well as cooked meals. Men and older boys worked in workshops or fields and constructed buildings. Meanwhile the Indian children went to school, where the padres taught them. After a noon meal there was a two hour rest before work began again. After dinner the Indians sang, played, or danced. This way of life was an enormous change from the less organized Indian life before the missionaries arrived. Many tribes accepted the change, some had more trouble getting used to a regular schedule, some tribes never became a part of mission life.

Water was all-important to the missions. It was needed to irrigate crops and to provide for the mission people and animals. Priests designed and engineered magnificent irrigation systems at most of the missions. All building of aqueducts and reservoirs of these systems was done by the mission Indians.

With all the organized hard work, the missions did very well. They grew and became strong. Excellent vineyards gave wine for the priests to use and to sell. Mission fields produced large grain crops of wheat and corn, and vast grazing land developed huge herds of cattle and sheep. Mission life was successful for over fifty years.

When Mexico broke away from Spain, it found it did not have enough money to support the California missions, as Spain had been doing. So in 1834, Mexico enforced the secularization law which their government had decreed several years earlier. This law stated missions were to be taken away from the missionaries and given to the Indians. The law said that if an Indian did not want the land or buildings, the property was to be sold to anyone who wished to buy it.

It is true the missions had become quite large and powerful. And as shocked as the padres were to learn of the secularization law, they also knew the missions had originally been planned as temporary, or short term projects. The priests had been sure their Indians would be well-trained enough to run the missions by themselves when the time came to move to other unsettled lands. In fact, however, even after fifty years the California Indians were still not ready to handle the huge missions.

Since the Indians did not wish to continue the missions, the buildings and land were sold, the Indians not even waiting for money or, in some cases, receiving money for the sale.

Sad times lay ahead. Many Indians went back to the old way of life. Some Indians stayed on as servants to the new owners and often these owners were not good to them. Mission buildings were used for everything from stores and saloons to animal barns. In one mission the church became a barracks for the army. A balcony was built for soldiers with their horses stabled in the altar area. Rats ate the stored grain and beautiful church robes. Furniture and objects left by the padres were stolen. People even stole the mission building roof tiles, which then caused the adobe brick walls to melt from rain. Earthquakes finished off many buildings.

Shortly after California became a part of the United States in the mid-1850s, our government returned all mission buildings to the Catholic Church. By this time most of them were in terrible condition. Since the priests needed only the church itself and a few rooms to live in, the other rooms of the mission were rented to anyone who needed them. Strange uses were found in some cases. In the San Fernando Mission, for example, there was once a pig farm in the patio area.

Tourists finally began to notice the mission ruins in the early 1900s. Groups of interested people got together to see if the missions could be restored. Some missions had been "modernized" by this time, unfortunately, but within the last thirty years historians have found enough pictures, drawings, and written descriptions to rebuild or restore most of the missions to their original appearances.

The restoration of all twenty-one missions is a splendid way to preserve our California heritage. It is the hope of many Californians that this dream of restoration can become a reality in the near future.

MISSION SAN FERNANDO REY de ESPAÑA

I. THE MISSION TODAY

Mission San Fernando is located on San Fernando Mission Boulevard in the city of San Fernando. When you come upon the mission, the only building you see is the original convento. There is not a church in sight. Behind the convento to the right is the mission quadrangle. The church is on the far side of the quadrangle patio, clear away from the main road.

This placement of buildings is most unusual for a mission. A convento was where the priests lived and usually they preferred having their living quarters near the church. It is only when you learn that San Fernando's convento was well known as an inn, or hotel, during mission days that you understand why it, not the church, was built beside the main road.

Mission San Fernando is beautifully cared for. The large patio has well-tended lawns and a flowing fountain in its center, although this is not an original fountain. The only remaining fountain of the two originals has been moved to a park across the street from the convento. It is built in the shape of a Moorish star and is a copy of an old fountain in Cordova, Spain. The mission's original soap works are also in this park.

Many excellent restorations have been completed on the quadrangle, but it is the well-preserved convento, or "Long Building" which is of greatest interest to those who search for bits of old mission life. The Long Building is well-named. It is 243 feet long and 50 feet wide, and is thought by some to be the largest mission building ever constructed. Twenty-one Roman arches form the corridor along the front of the convento. Although two stories high, only the lower level is open to the public. The giant double doors of the main entrance used to open onto the main room, or sala. This sala was the largest living room of any of the missions. The inside archways are cut in graceful Moorish designs; the walls are painted in fresco-style patterns.

11

Some of the rooms of the convento hold collections of objects of great value. One room contains 400 year old altar furnishings gilded in gold. Other rooms display everything from priests' robes to old paintings and an old pipe organ. A long room on one end of the Long Building was once used as a general store.

There are furnished bedrooms actually used by Father Fermin Lasuén, founder of the mission, and California's first bishop, Bishop Garcia Diego. One well-decorated guest room, rediscovered in 1933, is known to have been used by important governors and generals.

The restored kitchen for the entire mission is in this building, as is the winery and wine cellar. A huge stove covering one whole wall of the kitchen was used in cooking mission meals. The chimney of the stove was built big enough to also be used for smoking meats.

One of the most important rooms in the Long Building is the library containing old books of the mission padres. These 1,760 books have been moved often, and never really had a home until they were placed here in 1968. The story of the missions is held in this library.

The west end of the convento was used as an inn for travelers in mission days. Fine care was given to guests by the mission people. There is a special dining room at this end that was used to serve meals to guests.

One side of the mission quadrangle has been restored as a combination museum and workshop area. Although very little remains of Mission San Fernando itself, the museum shows fine examples of early California life. Separate workrooms have been furnished to show in detail how mission machinery and tools were used in mission days. A recently-built archives building has been placed just outside the quadrangle.

The present church is an exact replica of the 1806 church. The original church was lost in the recent 1971 earthquake. In true mission style, the building is 185 feet long and only 35 feet wide. The width of mission churches depended on the length of logs found nearby. The walls are of adobe brick and give one the feeling they are leaning inward. This may be partly true, but it is really because the walls are about five feet thick at the ground and taper to only three feet thick at the top. The roof of the church is tiled. A two-story bell tower near the front entrance of the church seems to be squashed between the restored quadrangle exterior and the church. It is built in the plain and simple style one finds in the church building.

Inside the church, to the left of the entrance, is the baptistry. A copy of the original copper font is in the center of this small room. On the walls of the church proper are French lithographs of the Stations of the Cross, brought from Mexico in 1941. The mission's original Stations of the Cross now hang in the museum at Mission San Gabriel. These painting are thought to be the oldest example of California Indian religious art. The church walls are fresco painted in busy Indian designs. Even the window wells are outlined in color. Eight false pillars placed evenly along the walls seem to divide the room into sections with their ornate trim.

In keeping with the rest of the church interior, the sanctuary has brightly painted reredos in colors of red, mustard yellow, black, and light blue. These natural colors were made by the Native Americans from herbs, berries, and roots. To the left of the main altar is a pulpit of decorated wood. On a ledge high above the main altar is the mission's handcarved wood statue of Saint Ferdinand III, patron saint of Mission San Fernando. The statue survived all the bad times of mission days, even the 1812 earthquakes, but during the 1971 earthquake this 500 year old statue fell onto the altar and parts of it were smashed to bits. It took an expert to piece the statue back together and to repaint the damaged areas so the original paint was matched.

Behind the north wall of the church is a small, pretty cemetery where over 2,000 people, most of them mission Indians, are buried. This tiny cemetery was used until 1917, but the last mission burial was in 1852.

II. HISTORY OF THE MISSION

Father Fermin Lasuén, then Father-presidente of the mission chain, founded Mission San Fernando Rey de España on September 8, 1797, in an oaken valley near Los Angeles. The mission was named for Saint Ferdinand III, King of Spain, who lived in the 1200s. San Fernando was the fourth mission

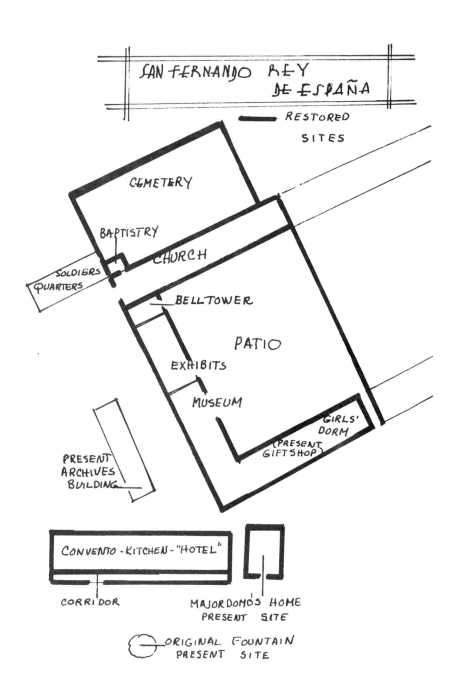

SAN FERNANDO REY
DE ESPAÑA

RESTORED SITES

CEMETERY

BAPTISTRY

CHURCH

SOLDIERS QUARTERS

BELLTOWER

PATIO

EXHIBITS

MUSEUM

GIRLS' DORM
(PRESENT GIFTSHOP)

PRESENT ARCHIVES BUILDING

CONVENTO - KITCHEN - "HOTEL"

CORRIDOR

MAJORDOMO'S HOME
PRESENT SITE

ORIGINAL FOUNTAIN
PRESENT SITE

Fr. Lasuén had founded that summer of 1797. The mission was supposed to have been placed farther north toward Mission Buenaventura, but this site had more water and the Indians were friendly. The man who "owned" the land, Don Francisco Reyes, mayor of Los Angeles, was asked to give the property to the missionaries. Since Senor Reyes probably did not really own the land, he had no choice but to give it to Father Lasuén for his mission.

Mission San Fernando was successful from the beginning. The first small chapel had to be replaced within a year of the founding because it had become too crowded. By 1804, nearly 1,000 Indians lived at San Fernando and the mission remained that size for at least twenty more years. In 1806, when the third church was dedicated, the entire quadrangle roof had been tiled and the mission contained soldier barracks, Indian homes, workshops, and storerooms within its walls.

Mission San Fernando was well-built, but not strong enough to remain standing through the 1812 earthquakes. The church walls were so badly damaged at that time thirty new beams were needed, along with a burned-brick buttress, to strengthen the building.

Work was begun on the convento in 1810. It took twelve years to build this large, beautiful structure. Unlike other mission conventos, this was not built next to the church, nor was it even a part of the quadrangle. It stood by itself on the main highway between Missions San Gabriel and Buenaventura, with the quadrangle and the church hidden behind it. When it was complete, it had a more majestic look to it than the mission church. Through the years the mission became famous for its convento inn. Several guest rooms were added when the second story was built in 1820. The mission was known to feed and "bed down" its guests for free, so the convento was always busy.

San Fernando's successful year was 1819. That year there were 12,800 cattle; 7,800 sheep; 176 goats; 45 pigs; 144 mules; and 780 horses recorded in the mission books. Cattle-raising was the biggest industry, but the mission was also known for its artistic wrought iron works. As with all missions, San Fernando natives produced soap, shoes, and animal hides. The Indian women here were particularly noted for a rough, serge-type cloth they wove. Adobe bricks and tile, carpentry products, and excellent baskets came from the mission workshops.

In the fields were huge vineyards of grapes used in making wine at the mission. The grapevines had originally come from Spain, but were brought north by the missionaries from the Baja missions in Mexico. Mission orchards grew all kinds of fruit. Records show that in 1832, 32,000 grapevines and 1,600 fruit trees were producing at Mission San Fernando.

There was trouble ahead for the mission, however. Mexico had broken away from Spain and was beginning to control California. Father Ibarra, a Spanish priest who stayed loyal to Spain, refused to go along with the new Mexican rule. He stayed at his Mission San Fernando until 1835, waiting to be replaced by a Mexican padre. When no one came to run the mission, Father Ibarra simply left the mission alone.

Secularization laws were now being strictly enforced, and the mission's downfall began. In 1842, the mayordomo who was sent from Mexico to manage the mission discovered gold on mission property. This was more than six years before the famous gold rush in northern California. It is agreed that some gold was found in areas near the mission, but the amount found near Sacramento completely overshadowed the San Fernando findings. For years afterward, however, gold prospectors thought the mission priests had gold buried in the church. Even as late as 1915, people were still digging up the floor of the ruined church, hunting for gold thought to be buried there by the padres.

The Mexican governor of California, Pio Pico, made Mission San Fernando his headquarters in 1846. Shortly before the United States took over California, Senor Pico sold the mission and the Indians all left. Governor Pico's brother continued to use the Long Building for his summer home for several years, but the mission church was completely abandoned in 1847. From 1857 to 1861 one end of the Long Building was a station for the Butterfield Stage Lines. In the late 1880s the Porter Land and Water Company used the west end for storerooms. The mission property was then used as a warehouse, a stable, and finally, in 1896, the poor quadrangle was actually used as a hog farm.

San Fernando's church became a working church again in 1923, when the Oblate priests arrived. The old church was repaired and served the people well until 1971, when it was damaged beyond repair by an earthquake. An exact replica was built and dedicated in 1974.

Although many attempts were made at restoration of the old mission from the early 1900s on, it was not until the Hearst Foundation gave a large gift of money to the mission in the 1940s that real restoration could begin. Today the church replica and other restorations are a fine tribute to the old mission days. As with many of the other active missions, Mission San Fernando will continue to repair and restore as needed. With constant care these monuments to California's past will never have to suffer from neglect again.

Flower-shaped fountain in center of restored quadrangle patio is copied from one in Cordova, Spain; is not original. One of two original fountains, a star-shaped one, was moved to the plaza across the street from the beautifully restored convento.

Interior of replica church, built after 1974 earthquake, has been called everything from "glorious" to "barbaric" with its wildly colored frescoed walls.

OUTLINE OF
MISSION SAN FERNANDO REY de ESPAÑA

I. **The mission today**
  A. Location
  B. First view of mission
    1. Convento
  C. Mission layout
    1. Church's location
  D. Good care of the mission
  E. Patio
    1. Fountains
  F. Convento building
    1. Size
    2. Outside corridor
    3. Main sala and doorways
    4. Collections
    5. Bedrooms of priests
    6. Kitchen
    7. Library
       a. Old mission books
    8. West end of convento
       a. Guest rooms
       b. Guest dining room
  G. Quadrangle
    1. Museum
    2. Workshops
  H. Church exterior
    1. Size
    2. Walls
    3. Bell tower
  I. Church interior
    1. Baptistry
    2. Stations of the Cross
       a. Originals at San Gabriel
    3. Wall designs
    4. Sanctuary
       a. Reredos
       b. Statue of St. Ferdinand
  J. Cemetery

Outline continued next page

II. History of the mission

A. Founding date
   1. Founder
B. Site change
   1. Francisco Reyes' gift
C. Success of the mission
   1. Buildings of 1806
D. 1812 earthquakes
E. Building of convento
   1. Second story added
F. Mission's best year
   1. Number of animals
   2. Indian products from workshops
G. Mission vineyards and orchards
H. Secularization problems
   1. Father Ibarra
I. San Fernando's small gold rush
J. Mission sold
   1. Governor Pico
K. Church abandoned
L. Uses of Long Building
   1. Butterfield Stage Lines
   2. Porter Land and Water Company
M. A hog farm in 1896
N. Oblate fathers in 1923
   1. Repairs
   2. 1971 earthquake
O. Restoration
   1. Hearst Foundation

GLOSSARY

BUTTRESS:	a large mass of stone or wood used to strengthen buildings
CAMPANARIO:	a wall which holds bells
CLOISTER:	an enclosed area; a word often used instead of convento
CONVENTO:	mission building where priests lived
CORRIDOR:	covered, outside hallway found at most missions
EL CAMINO REAL:	highway between missions; also known as The King's Highway
FACADE:	front wall of a building
FONT:	large, often decorated bowl containing Holy Water for baptizing people
FOUNDATION:	base of a building, part of which is below the ground
FRESCO:	designs painted directly on walls or ceilings
LEGEND:	a story coming from the past
PORTICO:	porch or covered outside hallway
PRESERVE:	to keep in good condition without change
PRESIDIO:	a settlement of military men
QUADRANGLE:	four-sided shape; the shape of most missions

RANCHOS:	large ranches often ...., from mission proper where crops were grown and animal herds grazed
REBUILD:	to build again; to repair a great deal of something
REPLICA:	a close copy of the original
REREDOS:	the wall behind the main altar inside the church
*RESTORATION:	to bring something back to its original condition (see * below)
SANCTUARY:	area inside, at the front of the church where the main altar is found
SECULARIZATION:	something not religious; a law in mission days taking the mission buildings away from the church and placing them under government rule
*ORIGINAL:	the first one; the first one built

BIBLIOGRAPHY

Bauer, Helen, *California Mission Days.* Sacramento, CA: California State Department of Education, 1957.

Goodman, Marian. *Missions of California.* Redwood City, CA: Redwood City Tribune, 1962.

Harrington, Marie. *Mission San Fernando.* Mission Hills, CA: San Fernando Valley Historical Society, Inc., 1981.

Sunset Editors. *The California Missions.* Menlo park, CA: Lane Publishing Company, 1979.

Weber, Msgr. Francis J. *San Fernando Mission.* pamphlet, n.d.

Wright, Ralph B., ed. *California Missions.* Arroyo Grande, CA 93420: Hubert A. Lowman, 1977.

For more information about this mission, write to:

Mission San Fernando Rey
15151 San Fernando Mission Blvd.
Mission Hills, CA 91345

It is best to enclose a self-adressed, stamped envelope and a small amount of money to pay for brochures and pictures the mission might send you.

CREDITS

Cover art and Father Serra Illustration: Ellen Grim
Illustrations: Alfredo de Batuc
Ground Layout: Mary Boulé